A Guide for Using

D1312279

The Magic School Bus® at the Waterworks

in the Classroom

Based on the book written by Joanna Cole

This guide written by Greg Young, M.S. Ed.

Teacher Created Resources

Teacher Created Resources, Inc.
6421 Industry Way
Westminster, CA 92683
www.teachercreated.com
©1996 Teacher Created Resources, Inc.
Reprinted, 2006
Made in U.S.A.
ISBN-1-57690-088-6

Edited by
Walter Kelly, M.A.

Illustrated by
Agi Palinay

Cover Art by
Dianne Birnbaum

Table of Contents

Introduction

The use of good trade books can enhance the study of science. The key to selecting these books is to check them for scientific accuracy and appropriateness for the level of the students. *The Magic School Bus®* series, written by Joanna Cole, contains outstanding examples of books which can help students learn about science and enjoy it. These books are delightfully written and scientifically accurate, thanks to the thorough research done by the author as she writes each of her books.

This **Science Literature Unit** is directly related to *The Magic School Bus® at the Waterworks.* The activities in this unit are particularly appropriate for intermediate grades. Teachers who use this unit will find a variety of lessons to do before, during, and after reading the book with their students. These include the following:

- Pre-reading Activity—Discovering initial knowledge of the way water works

- A Biographical Sketch and Picture of the Author

- A Book Summary

- Activity-oriented lessons which expand the topics covered in the story:

    - growing mold on bread
    - experimentally determining the amount of water in popcorn
    - graphically visualizing the distribution of water on our planet
    - observing the process of melting and boiling
    - extracting water from the atmosphere
    - forming clouds
    - creating a mural depicting the water cycle
    - creating a mural depicting the way water is purified
    - creating a replica of a water filtration plant
    - performing tests for water quality
    - investigating the fundamentals of siphon action
    - developing an effective water pistol

- Post-reading Activity—Creating a mural depicting how waste water is treated

- Unit Assessment—What Did You Learn?

- Annotated List of Books and Materials

- Answer Key

This unit is designed to help you present exciting lessons for your students so they can develop their understanding and appreciation of the function of water and its cycle in our everyday lives.

The Way Water Works

Before you begin reading *The Magic School Bus® at the Waterworks,* complete the following drawing and the series of questions on page 5. The final assessment will allow you to make a complete mural of the way water works and find the answers to these questions.

In the beginning of the book, Ms. Frizzle reminds the students of their upcoming trip to the waterworks. In preparation for the trip, she asks the students to research and record 10 facts about water. The students are not happy about conducting the research, but Ms. Frizzle is trying to prepare the students before embarking on their trip.

Directions for the pre-assessment:

Let's begin our own study of the way water works by seeing what you already know about it. Complete the drawing below. Notice there is a water pipe leading into the kitchen sink and a water pipe leaving the kitchen sink. Draw how you think the water gets into the faucet and where the water goes down the drain.

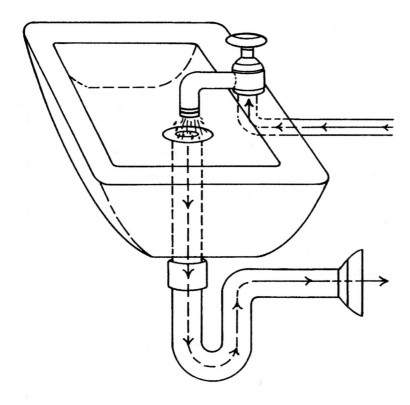

Water Questions

Pre-assessment Questions

Once you have completed your drawing of how water enters the faucet and where it goes after going down the drain, complete the following questions. If you are not sure of the answer, please write "I need more information." In this way, you can later compare what you already know to what you will learn about the way water works.

1. What role does water play in the popping of popcorn?

   _____

2. Is there more salt water or fresh water on the earth?

   _____

3. Is there water in the air that we breathe? How do you know?

   _____

4. How is a cloud formed? Include a drawing with your explanation.

5. Why do clouds stay in the air? Include a drawing with your explanation.

6. If you spill some water on the ground, where does the water go after a while? Include a drawing with your explanation.

7. If we "waste" water, will it disappear forever from the face of the earth? Explain what you mean.

   _____

   _____

   _____

   _____

About the Author

Joanna Cole was born on August 11, 1944, in Newark, New York. She attended the University of Massachusetts and Indiana University before receiving her B.A. from the City College of the City University of New York in 1967. She has worked as an elementary school library teacher and then as letters correspondent at *Newsweek.* Then she became senior editor of books for young readers at Doubleday & Co.

Ms. Cole has written over 20 books for children, most of which are nonfiction. Every writer begins his/her career somewhere; Joanna Cole's began with cockroaches. While working as a library teacher in a Brooklyn elementary school, her father gave her an article about cockroaches, telling how they were on Earth before the dinosaurs. She had enjoyed reading science books as a child and remembered finding books about insects to be the most fascinating to her. Since there were not any books about cockroaches, she decided to write one. Her first book, *Cockroaches,* was published in 1971.

Cole has written about fleas, dinosaurs, chicks, fish, saber-toothed tigers, frogs, horses, hurricanes, snakes, cars, puppies, insects, and babies, just to name a few examples. Ms. Cole knows that the important thing is to make the book so fascinating that the reader will be eager to go on to the next page.

Teachers and children have praised Ms. Cole's ability to make science interesting and understandable. Her *Magic School Bus*® series has now made science funny as well. Joanna says that before she wrote this series, she had a goal to write good science books told in a story that would be so much fun to read that readers would read it even without the science.

Readers across the country love *The Magic School Bus*® series and enjoy following the adventures of the wacky science teacher, Ms. Frizzle. Joanna Cole works closely with Bruce Degen, the illustrator for this series, to create fascinating and scientifically accurate books for children. Even a successful writer finds it sometimes scary to begin writing a new book. That was the way Cole felt before beginning to write *The Magic School Bus*® series. She says, "I couldn't work at all. I cleaned out closets, answered letters, went shopping—anything but sit down and write. But eventually I did it, even though I was scared."

Joanna Cole says kids often write their own *Magic School Bus*® adventures. She suggests they just pick a topic and a place for a field trip. Do a lot of research about the topic. Think of a story line and make it funny. Some kids even like to put their own teachers into their stories.

The Magic School Bus® *at the Waterworks*

by Joanna Cole

(Scholastic, 1986)

(Canada, Scholastic; U.K., Scholastic Limited; AUS, Ashton Scholastic Party Limited)

This year, the class has really bad luck. They get Ms. Frizzle as their teacher. She is known to be the strangest teacher in school. What they don't realize is that Ms. Frizzle enjoys taking her students on extravagant field trips they will not soon forget. Her field trips are designed to give the students a firsthand look at how something works, and in this case, how water works.

Before leaving on their trip, Ms. Frizzle asks her students to prepare a report containing 10 interesting facts about water. Most students don't believe there are 10 interesting facts about water. Little do they know there are many more than just 10. In fact, they are about to learn a whole lot more.

On the day of the field trip, Ms. Frizzle, wearing the octopus dress, rolls into the parking lot in her magic school bus. With some hesitation, the students board the bus and head off for their adventure. After passing through a dark tunnel, the bus is transformed into an ocean-going vessel, and the students are mysteriously outfitted with scuba gear.

Ms. Frizzle and her class are well on their way to learning about water. The bus is lifted into the atmosphere so the children may learn about cloud and rain formation. Following this discovery, the students and Ms. Frizzle fall to the earth as raindrops and flow into a reservoir. The class is following the path taken by water in what is known as the hydrologic, or water, cycle.

The class enters a pipe which takes them to the water purification system where they are subjected to cleaning and filtering as if they were impurities in the water. Since the class is too large to pass through the sand and gravel filters at the end of the process, they climb out of the filtration tank. Once outside the filtration tank, they see the water being cleaned by the chemicals fluoride and chlorine, being later pumped into a storage tank.

Before they know it, the class is swept out of the storage tank and into the pipes which carry the fresh water into the city. Flowing quickly through the underground water mains, Ms. Frizzle and her students ultimately enter a pipe which leads them back into their building. An unaware and startled seventh-grader turns on a faucet and lets the class out of the pipes and into the bathroom.

Upon drying off and returning to the classroom, Ms. Frizzle asks the students to make a chart which illustrates how water reaches their homes and buildings. The children ultimately create a wall chart which depicts the whole process they had witnessed firsthand. What a field trip!

Growing Mold Together

In the beginning of the book, Ms. Frizzle's students are just beginning to understand her unorthodox science teaching methods. Her methods are certainly not like those of the other teachers. In fact, Amanda Jane and Arnold find themselves growing mold together.

Ye Olde Moldy Oldy Experiment

Precaution

Never encourage students to "sniff" the mold with their noses. Bacteria can enter through the nasal passage. Be certain to wash hands with soap and water after touching bread, and dispose of bread in an airtight or outside receptacle.

Materials

a loaf of sliced bread, ziplock freezer bags, shoe box, magnifying lens(es), bowl of water, refrigerator (if available)

Questions Before You Begin

1. Have you ever seen bread with mold on it?

2. Do you think you should eat bread which has mold on it? Why or why not?

3. Under what conditions does bread seem to grow mold the fastest? (in a bright room, a dark room? a cold place, a warm place?)

4. How would you use the materials for this experiment to determine which conditions are most favorable for growing mold? (Use the table on page 9 to write your ideas.)

Procedure

1. List your ideas on the table on page 9. A few ideas are already listed to help you get started. If you need more room, write some more ideas on a separate sheet of paper.

2. Carry out your ideas. Be sure to start all the experiments at the same time.

Results

Over the next several days, observe and report on the progress of mold on your slices of bread. You should find that mold appears most quickly on those slices in dark, warm, damp areas.

Closure/Assessment

Design a package for bread and a label telling consumers how to store their bread to enhance its shelf life.

Bread Mold Table

Instructions: Three growing conditions have been suggested. Write at least seven more ideas and try them all. In the column on the right, write the date you first see bread mold on each piece of bread. As your mold grows, record its appearance by making a colored drawing. Be sure to include the date with each drawing.

Growing Condition	Date of First Mold	Appearance	Appearance	Appearance	Appearance
1. Place bread on the countertop.					
2. Place bread in a ziplock bag on countertop.					
3. Place bread in a dark closet.					
4.					
5.					
6.					
7.					
8.					
9.					
10.					

How Much Water Is in People?

Before Ms. Frizzle takes the students on a trip to the waterworks, she asks them to research *10 facts about water.* Her reason for this is to gather the students' current understanding of the way water works. Before taking any field trip, it is important to be prepared.

Water Fact #1: *About ²/₃ of your body is made up of water.*

As a Matter of Fact . . . Men typically have slightly more water in their bodies, pound for pound, than women. Men generally carry around one gallon (3.79 L) of water for every 12 ½ pounds of weight. Women carry around one gallon (3.79 L) of water for every 15 pounds of weight. This means the amount of water in a woman who weighs 100 pounds is 6.67 gallons (25.3 L) or 55.6 pounds of water! That should float your boat!

Math Break

❏ Your weight in pounds divided by 12 ½ (for males) or 15 (for females) will tell you how many gallons of water are in your body.

❏ Multiplying the number of gallons of water in your body by 8.33 will tell you how many pounds of water are in your body. Each gallon of water weighs about 8.33 pounds.

❏ Complete the chart on page 11 to determine the amount of water in your body.

Fun Fact:

During an average lifetime, a person will drink about 16,000 gallons (60,600 L) of water.

Finding Your Water Weight

English Units

Instructions: Write your weight in pounds in the space provided. Males will divide their weight by 12.5, and females will divide their weight by 15 to find the number of gallons of water in their bodies.

By multiplying the number of gallons of water in your body by 8.33, you can determine the weight of water in your body. Each gallon of water weighs 8.33 pounds.

Your Weight (lbs.)	Gallons of Water in Your Body (gal.)	Pounds of Water in Your Body (lbs.)
Male	lbs. ÷ 12.5 =	gal. x 8.33 =
Female	lbs. ÷ 15 =	gal. x 8.33 =

Metric Units

Instructions: Males will divide their mass by 1.5 while females will divide their mass by 1.8. By multiplying the number of liters of water in your body by 1, you can determine the mass of water in your body. Each liter of water has a mass of 1 kilogram.

Your Mass (kg.)	Liters of Water in Your Body (L)	Mass of Water in Your Body (kg)
Male	kg ÷ 1.5 =	L x 1 =
Female	kg ÷ 1.8 =	L x 1 =

How Much Water Is in Popcorn?

Popcorn pops because the water inside the hard kernel of corn is heated to boiling temperatures and literally bursts through the shell. The following activity is designed to measure how much water is inside a kernel of popcorn.

Materials

popcorn kernels, air popper (if possible), balance

Questions Before You Begin

1. Do you know what makes popcorn pop?

2. How would you use the materials for this activity to determine the amount of water in a kernel of popcorn?

Procedure

1. Using the balance, find the mass of 100 popcorn kernels.

2. Record their mass on the data table on page 13.

3. Place the popcorn kernels into the popcorn popper.

4. Pour some extra kernels into the popcorn popper as all 100 kernels may not pop.

5. When the popcorn is done popping, count out 100 popped pieces.

6. Find the mass of these popped pieces and record that number on the table on page 13.

7. Compare the mass of the popped pieces to the mass of the un-popped pieces.

Results

You should find the popped pieces have considerably less mass than the unpopped pieces.

Closure/Assessment

Complete the chart on page 13.

1. How many grams of water were in the unpopped kernels? _____

2. How did you figure this out? _____

3. How many grams of water were in each unpopped kernel?_____

4. How did you figure this out? _____

5. Using information from the table about your body (on page 11), determine how much of your weight is not water. _____

6. How did you figure this out? _____

Fun Fact: *Did you know that a popcorn kernel is about 13% water? When the kernels are heated to about 400° Fahrenheit (200° Celsius), the pressure inside each kernel forces it to pop. Popcorn kernels can pop to over 35 times their original size.*

Popcorn Chart

Instructions: Write the mass of 100 unpopped kernels of popcorn in the first space. After popping the popcorn, write the mass of 100 pieces of popped popcorn in the second space. By subtracting the two, you will find the mass of water which was in the unpopped kernels. Why? Because the water is what makes popcorn pop! When the kernels pop, they release the water trapped inside. The popped kernels are quite dry.

Mass of 100 Unpopped Kernels (grams)	−	Mass of 100 Popped Kernels (grams)	=	Mass of Water in Unpopped Kernels (grams)
____ g	−	____ g	=	____ g

To find the amount of water in *each* kernel, divide your answer by 100. Do you know why?

Mass of Water in Unpopped Kernels (grams)	÷ 100 =	Mass of Water in Each Kernel (grams)
____ g	÷ 100 =	____ g

How Is Water Distributed on Earth?

Wearing her octopus dress, Ms. Frizzle rolls the bus into the parking lot. Seeing this, the students are not too sure how well they are going to enjoy this trip. In fact, they become quite concerned when the Frizz drives the bus through a tunnel and they come out the other side wearing scuba gear!

Water Fact #2: *Water is the only substance that is found in the form of a liquid, a solid, and a gas in nature.*

As a Matter of Fact . . . Most of the earth's water is in the liquid form. Scientists estimate that 97.6% of the earth's water is a liquid while 2.39% is a solid and only 0.001% is a gas. Liquid water can be found in the oceans, rivers, lakes, streams, and even underground. Solid water (or ice) can be found in icebergs and glaciers. Gaseous water (or water vapor) can be found in the atmosphere.

What follows is an activity designed to illustrate how water is distributed on our planet. For purposes of this activity, we will imagine that a liter bottle (1000 mL) of water represents the entire supply of water on Earth.

Materials

graduated cylinder (able to hold at least 50 mL), 1 liter bottle of drinking water, 4 clear plastic cups, eyedropper, grease pencil

Questions Before You Begin

How many milliliters of water belong in each of the following categories? (You are just to make guesses here about how much water would actually be found in each category. Be sure your total does not exceed 1,000 mL.)*

1. _____ ocean

2. _____ icecaps and glaciers

3. _____ underground water

4. _____ lakes, rivers, streams

5. _____ atmosphere

        1000 mL   **Total**

* Why should the total amount not exceed 1,000 mL? _____

Once you have made your guesses as to how many milliliters would belong in each category, turn to the answer key on page 48 to see how close you were to the real values.

On the next page you will find the procedure for this activity. This will give you a visual representation of how the water is distributed on our planet.

How Is Water Distributed on Earth? *(cont.)*

Procedure

1. Using the grease pencil, mark each plastic cup with the following titles: "Icecaps and Glaciers," "Underground Water," "Lakes, Rivers, Streams," and "Atmosphere."

2. Measure out 23 mL from the 1 liter of water in a graduated cylinder.

3. Pour the 23 mL into the plastic cup marked "Icecaps and Glaciers."

4. Measure out 4 mL from the 1 liter of water in a graduated cylinder.

5. Pour the 4 mL into the plastic cup marked "Underground Water."

6. Remove 2 drops from the 1 liter of water and place them into the plastic cup marked "Lakes, Rivers, Streams."

7. Remove 1 drop from the liter of water and place it into the plastic cup marked "Atmosphere."

Closure/Assessment

Follow the instructions for making the tables and graphs for this activity on pages 16 and 17. When you have completed the tables and graphs, answer the following questions:

1. What percent of the earth's water is in icecaps and glaciers?

   _____

2. What percent of the earth's *fresh* water is in icecaps and glaciers?

   _____

3. What percent of the earth's *fresh* water is in lakes, rivers, and streams?

   _____

4. On the pie chart, what angle was used to represent underground water?

   _____

Fun Fact: *Did you know that our earth holds some 300 million cubic miles of water? All of the earth's water would fit into a bottle 670 miles tall, 670 miles wide, and 670 miles deep! That is enough water to cover the entire United States to a depth of 100 miles!*

Bar Graph:
Amounts of Fresh Water on Earth

Instructions: Look at the answer key on page 48. Look only at the answers for page 14 for the section entitled "Questions Before You Begin." Using those answers, fill in the table below.

_____ mL of water in icecaps and glaciers

_____ mL of water underground

_____ mL of water in lakes, rivers, and streams

_____ mL of water in the atmosphere

Task: Using the grid below, make a bar graph which represents the amount of fresh water found in each of the following areas: (1) Icecaps and Glaciers, (2) Underground, (3) Lakes, Rivers, and Streams, (4) Atmosphere

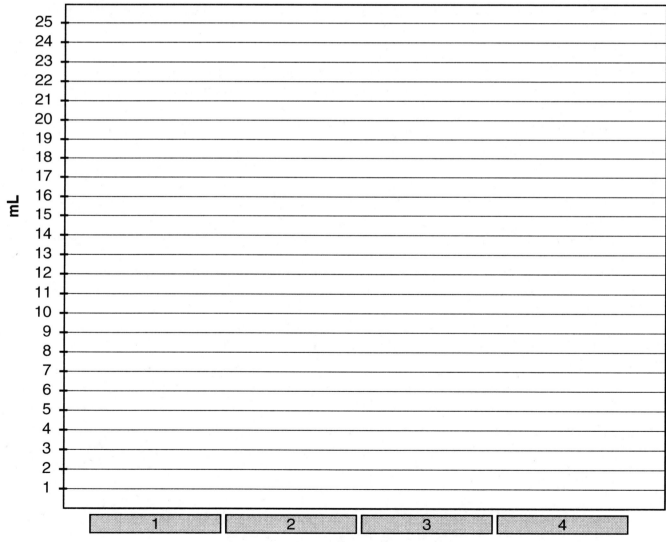

Areas Containing Fresh Water

Pie Graph:
Amounts of Fresh Water on Earth

Task: Compute the percentage of fresh water in each of the following areas: (1) Icecaps and Glaciers, (2) Underground, (3) Lakes, Rivers, and Streams, (4) Atmosphere.

How to Do It: Divide each of the four areas' volumes of fresh water by the total volume of all the fresh water on Earth at this scale (that would be 28 mL total). Round each answer to the nearest tenth. Then, multiply each answer by 100 to find the percentage of water in each area.

_____ ÷ 28 mL = _____ x 100 = _____ % Icecaps/Glaciers

_____ ÷ 28 mL = _____ x 100 = _____ % Underground

_____ ÷ 28 mL = _____ x 100 = _____ % Lakes/Rivers/Streams

_____ ÷ 28 mL = _____ x 100 = _____ % Atmosphere

Task: Copy the values from the column with the box around it to the column on the left below this task. Multiply these values by 360—the number of degrees in a circle. This will give you the number of degrees each area will cover inside the circle. Round the values to the nearest whole degree.

_____ x 360° = _____ ° Icecaps/Glaciers

_____ x 360° = _____ ° Underground

_____ x 360° = _____ ° Lakes/Rivers/Streams

_____ x 360° = _____ ° Atmosphere

How to make your pie chart: On the next page, use a protractor to help you divide the circle into the four areas containing fresh water. Label and color each area.

Pie Graph:
Amounts of Fresh Water on Earth

(cont.)

Instructions: Using a protractor, divide the circle into segments representing the number of degrees

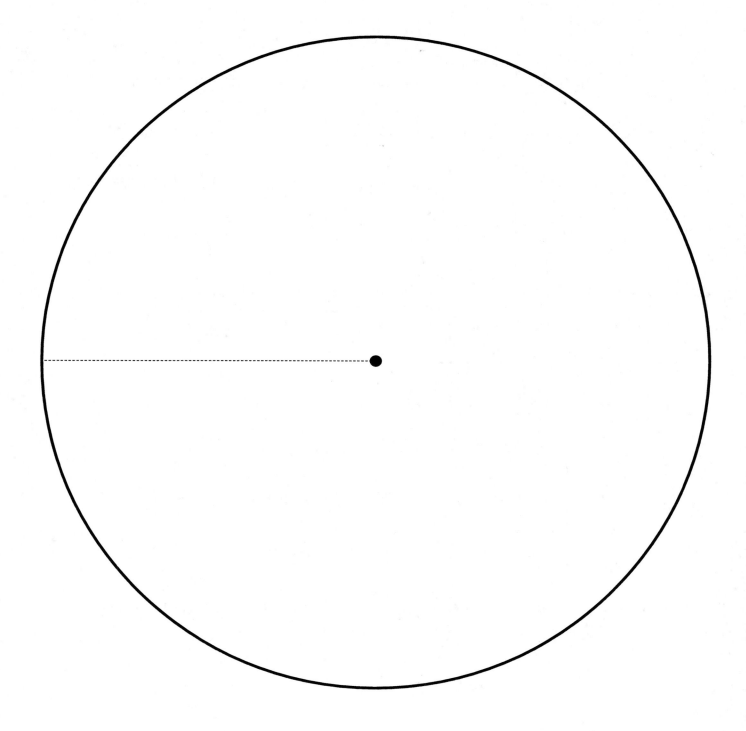

Melting the Cube

Materials

ice cube, cooking pot, stove, stopwatch

Questions Before You Begin

1. How long will it take an ice cube to melt on the stove? Record your guess on page 20.

2. How long will it take the melted ice cube to then boil? Record your guess on page 20.

Procedure

1. Place an ice cube in the pot and turn on the stove.

2. Use a watch to time the ice cube as it melts.

3. Record this time on page 20.

4. Use the watch to then record the amount of time it takes the melted ice to boil.

5. Record this time page on 20.

6. Continue boiling the water until it completely boils away.

Preview of Coming Attractions

The next activity will actually bring water back from the air!

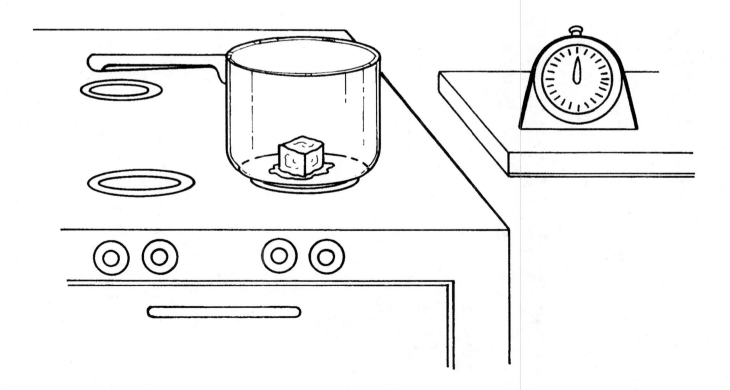

Melting the Cube Data Sheet

Instructions: In the boxes on the left side of the data sheet, place your predictions for how long it will take an ice cube to melt and how long it will take a melted ice cube to boil. Record the actual times in the boxes to their right. How close were your predictions?

Use the boxes on the extreme right side to draw a melting ice cube and boiling water.

	Predicted Time	Actual Time	Appearance
Melting			
Boiling			

Closure/Assessment

1. Where did the water go after it boiled away? _____

_____

_____

2. Is the water gone forever? Explain. _____

_____

_____

Water in the Air

After leaving the tunnel, the bus slowly begins to rise into the air. The class is now following the path water takes when the sun warms it into a vapor to form clouds. Arnold knew he should have stayed home today!

Water Fact #3: *There is water in the air you are breathing. You can't see it because it is in the form of an invisible gas called water vapor.*

As a Matter of Fact . . . There is 10 times more water in the earth's atmosphere than in all the rivers in the world.

The Dew Point of Air

One way to illustrate the fact that the air contains water vapor is to breathe on a mirror or window. You will literally be able to see your breath.

Materials

mirror or window

Procedure

Breathe on the window or mirror.

The Dew Point of Air

Not only is there water in your breath, there is also water in the air. This demonstration is designed to illustrate the existence of water in the earth's atmosphere.

Materials

empty coffee can, thermometer, ice, water, food dye

Questions Before You Begin

1. Have you ever seen dew in the morning?

2. What causes dew?

Scientific Explanation

Dew forms when the outside air temperature becomes cold enough to turn the water vapor in the air back into a liquid. Dew formation can also happen indoors if you cool a portion of the air enough to change the water vapor back into a liquid. We call this *liquid dew*. And the temperature at which the water vapor begins to form into dew is known as the *dew point*.

Procedure

1. Fill the coffee can halfway to the top with water.

2. Place a few drops of food dye in the coffee can.

3. Place the thermometer in the coffee can.

4. Begin to add ice slowly to the coffee can.

5. Watch the outside of the coffee can for signs of "sweating."

6. Immediately record the temperature when you see "sweating." This is the dew point.

Closure/Assessment

1. Did the "sweat" which formed on the outside of the can come through the coffee can?

2. How do you know your answer to number 1 is correct?

3. Where else have you seen a phenomenon similar to this?

4. Would you expect to find dew on the outside of a hot cup of cocoa or coffee?

5. Why does the bathroom mirror sometimes fog up when you take a hot shower or bath?

6. Why won't cold water baths or showers cause dew to form on the mirror?

Fun Fact: *Airports always include the temperature and the dew point in their weather reports. Pilots know that if by late afternoon temperatures are only a few degrees warmer than the dew point, fog is probably going to form by morning.*

Cloud in a Bottle

You can simulate the conditions of the upper atmosphere on warm, moist air with a demonstration known as "the cloud in the bottle."

Materials

two-liter plastic soda bottle, rubbing alcohol (or water), bicycle pump, ball-pump needle, rubber stopper, transparency of cloud formation on page 25

Preparation

Before performing this demonstration, prepare the rubber stopper in the following manner: Insert the ball-pump needle into the wide end of the stopper and press it through to the other end. Be certain the rubber stopper will fit snugly into the mouth of the two-liter plastic soda bottle.

Question Before You Begin

Describe the process of basic cloud formation. (Use the transparency of cloud formation on page 25 as a guide.)

Safety Precaution: Goggles should be worn as a precaution.

Procedure

1. Pour about a tablespoon of rubbing alcohol into the bottle. (Water will also work, but not as well as rubbing alcohol.)

2. Stopper the bottle and attach the bicycle pump to the needle.

3. Have a helper hold the stopper in place as you pump.

4. After 3–5 pumps, ask your helper to remove the stopper.

Results: A white fluffy cloud will form in the bottle. Essentially, you have simulated the behavior of water vapor in the upper atmosphere. As the pressure in the bottle rapidly decreased due to the rapid escape of air, the alcohol vapor (or water vapor) was forced to quickly expand. This rapid expansion caused the vapor to cool quickly and form cloud droplets.

Alcohol will form a cloud with less pressure reduction than will water. Therefore, alcohol is recommended but not essential for this demonstration.

Extension of Activity: By replacing the stopper in the bottle and applying pressure, see if you can make the cloud disappear. The demonstration can be repeated many times.

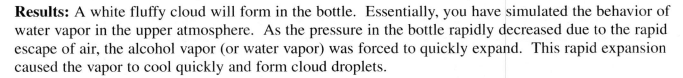

Fun Fact: *Rain droplets are about 100 times larger than cloud droplets. A rain droplet forms when a hundred or more cloud droplets attach themselves to a particle of dust or ice within the cloud. At this point, the water droplets are heavy enough to fall towards the earth as either rain or snow.*

Clouds

The school bus delivers the class to the clouds. As the students walk around outside of the bus, they notice that the clouds are made of water and the temperature is quite cold. Ultimately the students shrink to the size of raindrops and begin to fall toward the earth.

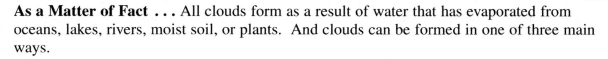

Water Fact #4: *Clouds are water. The higher up you go, the colder the air is. When water vapor rises, the cold air makes the vapor form droplets which hang in the air as a mist. This is a cloud.*

As a Matter of Fact . . . All clouds form as a result of water that has evaporated from oceans, lakes, rivers, moist soil, or plants. And clouds can be formed in one of three main ways.

1. **Convection:** When the sun warms the ground, the air above the ground is heated and begins to rise. This warm air, containing water vapor, rises in a process known as *convection*.

   Since the upper atmosphere has less pressure than the lower atmosphere, the rising air and water vapor will expand and become cooler. The cooling water vapor forms a fog. Fogs which are high above the ground are called *clouds*.

2. **Lifting:** Clouds are formed by lifting when warm, moist air moves up the side of a mountain. Along its journey, the air is lifted higher into the atmosphere where the pressure is lower. Again, the water vapor in the air is allowed to cool and form a fog. This is why we often see clouds over mountains.

3. **Frontal Activity:** Sometimes a mass of warm, moist air, known as a *warm front*, will run into a mass of colder air, known as a *cold front*. When the two meet, the warm, moist air rises higher into the atmosphere. The lower pressure of the upper atmosphere causes the water vapor in the warm air to cool and form a cloud.

Cloud Formation in a Nutshell

All three methods of cloud formation share the same attributes:

1. Warm, moist air rises into the upper atmosphere.

2. The upper atmosphere has lower air pressure than the lower atmosphere.

3. Under the conditions of lower air pressure, the warm air cools and forms clouds.

Clouds *(cont.)*

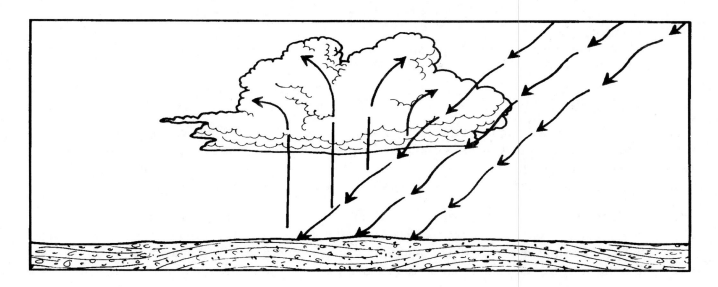

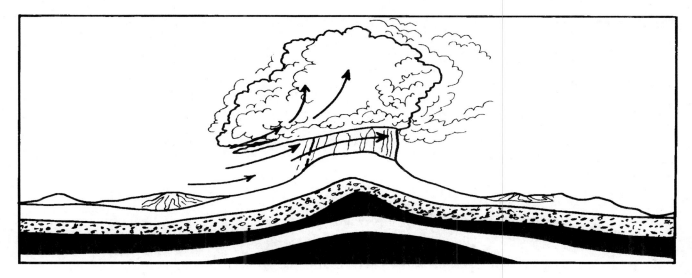

How Do Clouds Float While Raindrops Fall?

Ms. Frizzle and her students shrink to the size of raindrops and fall toward the earth. Perhaps you are wondering why raindrops fall toward the earth but clouds remain in the sky.

Scientific Explanation

The reason cloud droplets remain in the sky while raindrops fall is that they have different sizes and weights. Since a typical rain droplet is 100 times larger than a typical cloud droplet, it is also heavier. Both rain and cloud particles are droplets of water. They look exactly the same but are different sizes. Think of how a grain of sand is similar in shape—but not size—to a boulder, and you will get the idea.

Gravity pulls equally on cloud droplets and rain droplets, but since the earth has an atmosphere, an effect called *air resistance* slows down the speeds of falling objects. Air resistance has a greater effect on the speed of the smaller cloud droplet than of the larger rain droplet. The following activity is designed to illustrate this concept of air resistance and its effect on clouds and rain.

Materials

spray bottle with pump, water, eyedropper, paper, book, balance

Questions Before You Begin

1. Do all objects fall toward the earth at the same speed?

2. For example, if you dropped a feather and a rock simultaneously, would they both strike the ground at the same time?

Procedure (Part 1)

1. Using the spray bottle, spray a fine mist of water into the air. Notice how much of the mist seems to "hang" in the air for a while before falling.

2. Use the eyedropper to release drops of water towards the ground. Notice that none of the water drops appear to hang in the air before falling to the ground.

Results: You can clearly see that the smaller particles in the mist were affected by air resistance more than the drops of water were.

Closure/Assessment

Why do you think the mist seems to hang in the air for a while but the dripping water does not?

_____

_____

_____

_____

How Do Clouds Float While Raindrops Fall? *(cont.)*

Procedure (Part 2)

1. Weigh the piece of paper on a balance (do not fold or crumple the paper when finding its mass).

2. Record the mass of the paper.

3. Drop the paper and the book simultaneously from the same height. Watch as the book strikes the ground first.

4. Now, crumple the paper into a tight wad and repeat the dropping exercise. Notice how the paper falls more closely with the book.

5. Weigh the crumpled piece of paper to see that it is the same mass as before.

Results: You should see that not only does weight affect air resistance, but so does surface area. The flat paper is more affected by air resistance than the crumpled paper is. Similarly, a spherical raindrop falls to earth much faster than would a flat raindrop.

Closure/Assessment

1. Why do you think parachutes are shaped the way they are?

   _____

   _____

   _____

2. Since there is no air on the moon, would the astronauts be able to parachute from their space ship to the lunar surface? Why or why not?

   _____

   _____

   _____

Fun Fact: *Because of gravity and air resistance, clouds are constantly falling toward the earth at an average speed of 0.02 miles per hour. At that rate, it would take 7–8 days before a cloud would hit the ground. Raindrops, however, fall at a rate close to 14 miles per hour. Raindrops strike the ground nearly 15 minutes after they fall from a cloud.*

The Water Cycle

The class, which has now turned into a group of raindrops, lands in a clear mountain stream. After landing, Ms. Frizzle leads the students down the stream and into a local reservoir.

Water Fact #5: *There is exactly the same amount of water on Earth now as there was millions of years ago. The water keeps going around and around. It evaporates from lakes, rivers, and oceans, and forms clouds in the sky. Then it returns to Earth again as rain or snow. This process is called the* water cycle.

As a Matter of Fact . . . Each day, over 275 trillion gallons of water evaporate from the surface of the earth into the atmosphere. That's over 3 billion gallons per second!

Materials

bucket, water, chalk

Procedure

1. On a warm day, go outside to a patch of asphalt.
2. Throw a bucketful of water onto the asphalt.
3. Using a piece of chalk, trace the outside boundaries of the puddle.
4. Return to the classroom.
5. Throughout the day, return to the puddle to trace the outside boundaries.

Closure/Assessment

1. What will the puddle look like when you return to check on it in a short while?

_____

_____

_____

2. Where will the water go?

_____

_____

_____

Make Your Own Water Cycle

Materials

pot of water, hot plate or stove, food dye, salt, plastic salad bowl (clear if possible), ice cubes, plastic bag, oven mitt

Questions Before You Begin

1. When you poured water on the hot asphalt, what caused the water to turn into steam?

2. Now, can you speed up the process by placing some water to boil on a hot plate?

Procedure

1. Pour some water into the pot and set the pot on the hot plate (or stove) to boil.

2. Put on your oven mitt.

3. As the water boils, invert the salad bowl over the steam to catch the vapors.

4. Placing ice cubes in a plastic bag above the salad bowl will help condense the steam back into a liquid.

ice

condensation   salad bowl

Results: The vapor will collect and condense inside the bowl.

Extension: Repeat the experiment; only this time, mix some salt in with the water. Before boiling, test the salt water by dipping a finger into it and taking a taste. After collecting the condensation in the salad bowl, taste the condensate by running your finger along the inside of the bowl and tasting your finger. Is it still salty?

Or, place a few drops of food coloring in the water before boiling. Do you believe the condensation will also be colored?

Results: The process of boiling the water into a vapor will remove most of the impurities such as salt and food color. This helps illustrate the cleansing power of the water cycle.

> **Fun Fact:** *The earth's oceans would completely evaporate in about 4000 years if it were not for the fact that the water is ultimately returned through rain.*

The Water Cycle Travelogue

Fueled by the energy of the sun, the water cycle is the process through which nature recycles the earth's water supply. No one knows where the cycle starts or where it ends; it is continuous. What follows is a description of the process, step by step. Read the following sections, and identify their individual parts on the diagram provided on page 32.

1. Evaporation

The sun's energy causes the water in the oceans, lakes, rivers, soil, and plants to heat up and vaporize. Much like steam rising from a pot of boiling water, this water vapor will slowly rise into the upper atmosphere and form clouds.

Of the 91,000 cubic miles (380,000 cubic kilometers) of water evaporated each year, 83% comes from the oceans, and 17% comes from the land. In fact, each year, the sun successfully evaporates a 3.3 foot (1 meter) layer of the ocean's surface. At this rate, the entire ocean could be evaporated in a little over 4000 years! The reason why the ocean doesn't evaporate, however, is because of . . .

2. Precipitation

What goes up, must come down. The 91,000 cubic miles (380,000 cubic kilometers) of water evaporated each year is returned to the earth in the form of rain and snow. This rain and snow is composed of fresh water which has had most of the elements and impurities (such as salt) removed.

When water falls on the earth, it is used for a variety of purposes: snow in the mountains, refilling lakes, watering plants, powering generators, and providing drinking water for people and animals. Once the water has been used, it is returned to the water cycle. Believe it or not, you may be drinking water which once passed through a dinosaur! Yuck!

The Water Cycle Travelogue *(cont.)*

The following is a continuation of the description begun on page 30. These are steps three and four of the process through which nature recycles the earth's water supply.

3. Wetlands

When dinosaurs roamed the earth (and even today), nature provided a system of treatment for animal wastes. For millions of years, the wetlands of the world have provided a filtering treatment for waste water before it is returned to the water cycle. Wetlands are areas close to bodies of water such as rivers, lakes, and oceans. Wetlands filter the sediments and nutrients created by animal and geologic waste. By filtering the water, the wetlands reduce the amount of waste and sediment poured directly into lakes, rivers, and oceans. But wetlands cannot do the job alone.

4. Waste Water Treatment Facilities

Since the early 1900s, it has become essential for humans to create their own artificial wetlands. Since many people often live in large communities near bodies of water, their collected waste water would overload nature's wetland system. These artificial wetlands created by people are known as waste water treatment facilities.

Each year, over 15,000 waste water treatment facilities in the United States treat several billions of gallons of waste water sewage. After treatment, the cleaner water is returned to the environment. Clean as it is, however, nature provides the final cleansing through evaporation and precipitation. The cycle continues.

Make a Chart

Instructions: Make an overhead transparency of the following picture of the water cycle. Place the transparency on an overhead projector and project the image on a large piece of butcher paper. Trace and color the image. Hang your poster in your room.

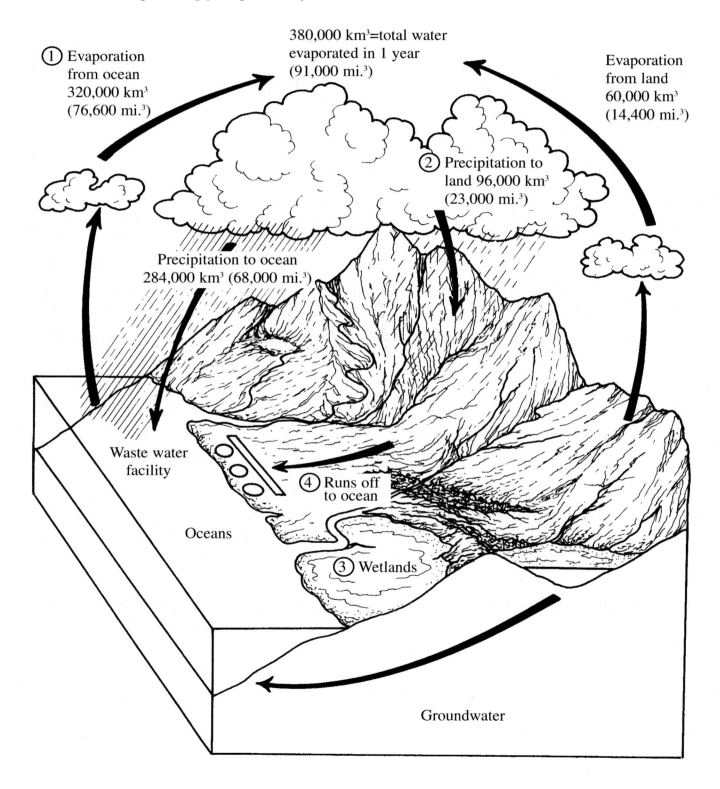

Rendezvous at the Reservoir

After Ms. Frizzle and her students become raindrops and fall back to Earth, they rendezvous at a reservoir. Now Ms. Frizzle's class will learn how communities collect, clean, and distribute water to people.

Water Fact #6: *Less than one percent of all the water on earth is fresh water that we can drink. The rest is salty water in the oceans or frozen water in glaciers or ice caps.*

As a Matter of Fact . . . Over 70% of the earth's fresh water supply is locked up in the Antarctic ice cap. Of the remaining fresh water, only 38% of it is accessible for us to use. This means we can collect, process, and distribute only 0.0026% of the world's entire (salt and fresh) water supply. Literally, a drop in the bucket!

Water Filtration Activity

Materials

1000 mL of muddy water, activated charcoal (available at pet stores), gravel, fine sand, cheesecloth, string, 2-liter soda bottle, cup, ring stand

Procedure

1. Prepare your soda bottle by cutting off the bottom.
2. Invert the bottle into the ring stand so that the mouth points down.
3. Tie a piece of cheesecloth over the mouth of bottle.
4. Pour a 1" (2.5 cm) layer of activated charcoal into the bottle.
5. Pour a 3" (7.5 cm) layer of fine sand over the activated charcoal.
6. Fill the rest of the bottle with gravel.
7. Place the cup beneath the mouth of the bottle.
8. Slowly pour the muddy water into the bottle and watch what happens.

Results: The gravel will remove the largest particles, the sand will remove some of the smaller particles, and the charcoal will provide the final filtration. Much of the water will be absorbed by the sand and charcoal, but enough should pass through the cheesecloth to provide you with a clear water product.

Caution: DO NOT DRINK THE FINAL PRODUCT! *(Harmful bacteria could still be present.)*

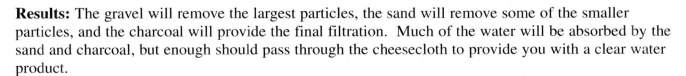

Fun Fact: *The average American uses about 80 gallons (300 L) of water each day, 60 gallons (225 L) of which are used in the bathroom!*

How We Get Our Water

As Ms. Frizzle's class discovers, fresh water is gathered in an artificial lake known as a *reservoir*. The water is then cleaned and filtered before entering our homes. What follows is a description of this process from start to finish. Read the travelogue and follow along with the diagram on page 35.

1. Aeration

From the reservoir, water is transported through pipes to an aeration tank. Here, water is sprayed into the air to release any trapped gases and absorb additional oxygen for better taste.

2. Coagulation

Next, the water heads off to the coagulation tanks to begin a three-step process of dirt removal. At this point, a chemical called *alum* is added to the water and breaks down into tiny, sticky particles called *floc*. The floc causes dirt to coagulate and settle towards the bottom as it becomes heavier.

3. Sedimentation

After being coagulated, the water is sent off to the sedimentation tanks. Sedimentation is the second step in the dirt removal process. The sedimentation tanks allow the dirt to settle to the bottom while cleaner water remains on the top and can flow on to the filtration step. This is why the entry and exit pipes to the sedimentation tanks are located at the top.

4. Filtration

Water coming from the sedimentation tanks now enters the third and final process of dirt removal. Even after depositing dirt in the sedimentation tank, there is still some dirt left in the water. The water is now filtered through charcoal, sand, and gravel at the bottom of the filtration tank and is sent off to be chlorinated and fluoridated.

5. Chlorinating/Fluoridation

At this point, most of the dirt has been removed from the water. Now, a chemical called *chlorine* is added to kill any bacteria left in the water. A chemical called *fluoride* is also sometimes added in an effort to improve the quality of teeth in the people who will be drinking the water.

6. Storage Tanks

Finally, the cleaned, filtered, and chemically treated water is held in storage tanks to be distributed to farms, homes, and businesses through a network of canals and pipes.

> **Fun Fact:** *The world's largest water treatment plant is Chicago's Central Water Filtration Plant located on a man-made peninsula in Lake Michigan. It supplies the 2.8 million people in Chicago and its nearby suburbs with over 1.5 billion gallons (5.7 billion liters) of water per day.*

How-We-Get-Our-Water Chart

Instructions: Make an overhead transparency of the following picture of a water filtration plant. Place the transparency on an overhead projector and project the image on a large piece of butcher paper. Trace and color the image. Hang your poster in your room.

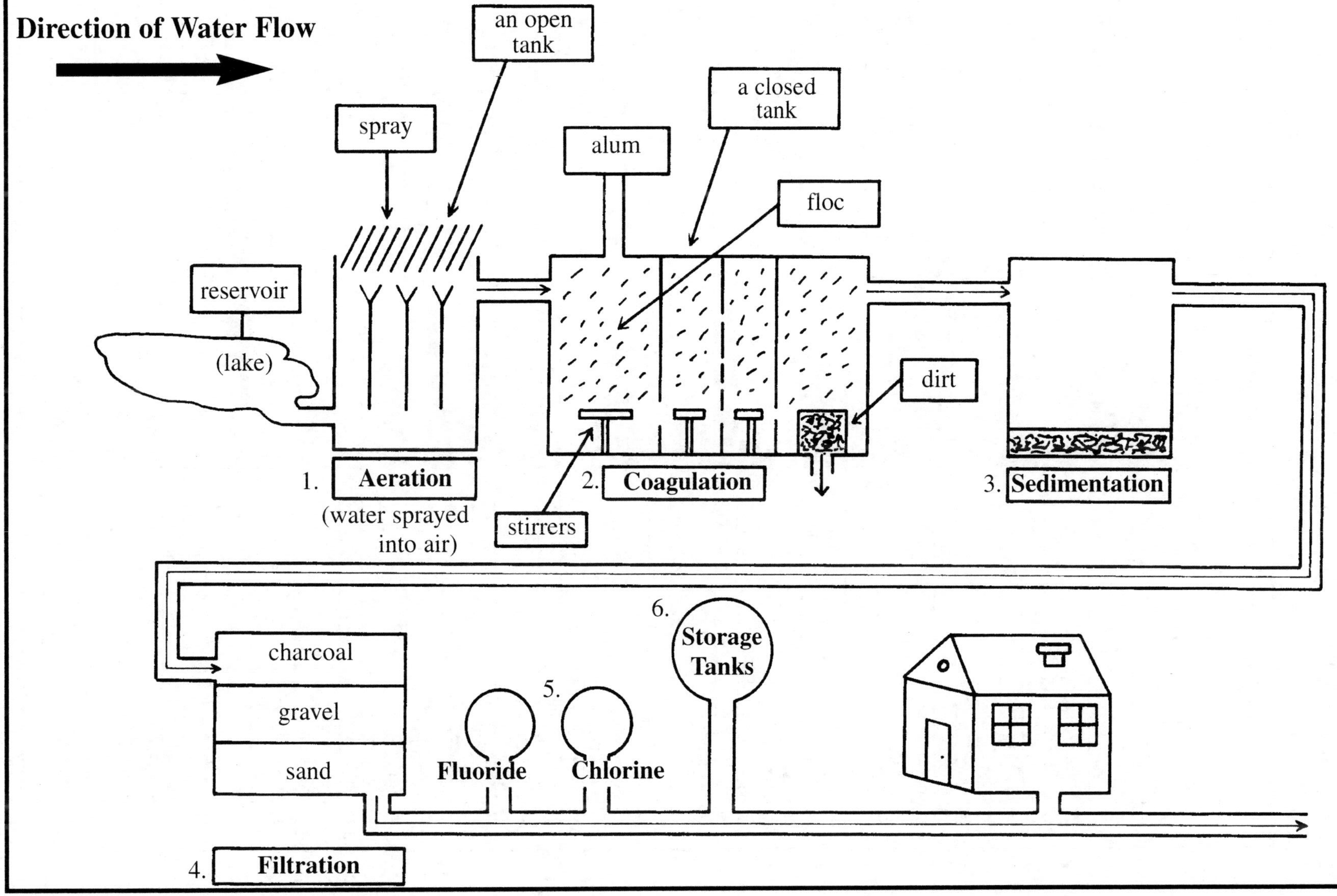

Direction of Water Flow

reservoir

(lake)

spray

an open tank

1. Aeration
(water sprayed into air)

alum

a closed tank

floc

stirrers

2. Coagulation

dirt

3. Sedimentation

charcoal

gravel

sand

Fluoride   **Chlorine**

5.

6. **Storage Tanks**

4. Filtration

Freshwater Use

To the Teacher: The following statistics are from the U.S. Geological Survey. The questions which follow are for individuals or groups.

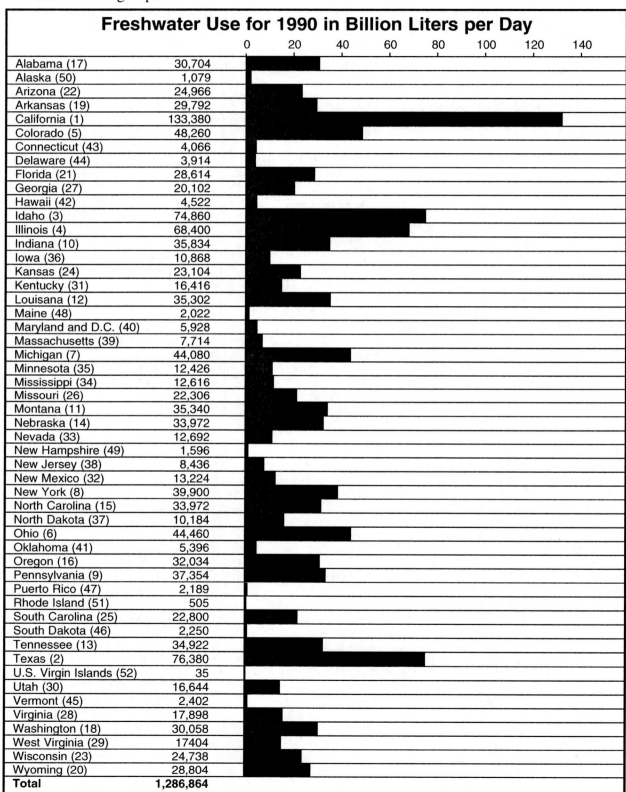

Freshwater Use for 1990 in Billion Liters per Day

Alabama (17)	30,704
Alaska (50)	1,079
Arizona (22)	24,966
Arkansas (19)	29,792
California (1)	133,380
Colorado (5)	48,260
Connecticut (43)	4,066
Delaware (44)	3,914
Florida (21)	28,614
Georgia (27)	20,102
Hawaii (42)	4,522
Idaho (3)	74,860
Illinois (4)	68,400
Indiana (10)	35,834
Iowa (36)	10,868
Kansas (24)	23,104
Kentucky (31)	16,416
Louisana (12)	35,302
Maine (48)	2,022
Maryland and D.C. (40)	5,928
Massachusetts (39)	7,714
Michigan (7)	44,080
Minnesota (35)	12,426
Mississippi (34)	12,616
Missouri (26)	22,306
Montana (11)	35,340
Nebraska (14)	33,972
Nevada (33)	12,692
New Hampshire (49)	1,596
New Jersey (38)	8,436
New Mexico (32)	13,224
New York (8)	39,900
North Carolina (15)	33,972
North Dakota (37)	10,184
Ohio (6)	44,460
Oklahoma (41)	5,396
Oregon (16)	32,034
Pennsylvania (9)	37,354
Puerto Rico (47)	2,189
Rhode Island (51)	505
South Carolina (25)	22,800
South Dakota (46)	2,250
Tennessee (13)	34,922
Texas (2)	76,380
U.S. Virgin Islands (52)	35
Utah (30)	16,644
Vermont (45)	2,402
Virginia (28)	17,898
Washington (18)	30,058
West Virginia (29)	17404
Wisconsin (23)	24,738
Wyoming (20)	28,804
Total	**1,286,864**

Freshwater Use *(cont.)*

Area Use (per day)—1990

Agriculture	535.80 billion liters
Thermoelectric Power	497.80 billion liters
Domestic and Commercial	148.58 billion liters
Industrial and Mining	105.64 billion liters

Individual Household Use (per person per day)—1990

Landscaping	49 gallons	(%)
Toilets	27 gallons	(%)
Showers/Baths	25 gallons	(%)
Laundry	19 gallons	(%)
Cooking/Cleaning	11 gallons	(%)
Dishwashing	5 gallons	(%)
Total	137 gallons	(%)

Questions for Students

1. Without looking a the statistics, can you think of which states (and U.S. provinces of the Virgin Islands and Puerto Rico) are in the top 10 of water use each year? Why do you think your choices are correct?

   Now look at the statistics. Were you correct? Why do you think those states are the top 10? Look up these states in an encyclopedia and see whether you can find reasons for their using so much water.

2. Without looking at the statistics, can you think of which states (and U.S. provinces of the Virgin Islands and Puerto Rico) are in the bottom 10 of water use each year? Why do you think your choices are correct?

   Now look at the statistics. Were you correct? Why do you think those states are the bottom 10? Look up these states in an encyclopedia and see whether you can find reasons for their using so little water.

3. The U.S. Geological Survey breaks up water use into four major categories: domestic and commercial, industrial and mining, thermoelectric power, and agricultural. List these four categories in order of their use of water, from biggest user to smallest user.

4. Before looking at the statistics, list the following residential uses of water in order from greatest to least: showers/baths, laundry, cooking/cleaning, toilets, dishwashing, landscaping. Check your answers against the statistics.

5. Look at the statistics for the number of gallons of water used per day per person. What percentage of the water is used for landscaping? for toilets? for showers/baths? for laundry? for cooking/cleaning? for dishwashing?

Testing Water Quality

The students and Ms. Frizzle become fluoridated and chlorinated. They are learning how chemicals can be useful in controlling and eliminating germs in their drinking water.

> **Water Fact #7:** *Clear water is not always clean water. It may still contain disease germs that can make you sick.*
>
> **As a Matter of Fact . . .** Water, even bottled water, is never pure H_2O. There are always some impurities such as salt and minerals in the water. In 1974, the United States Congress passed the Safe Drinking Water Act in an effort to reduce the amount of harmful bacteria, metals, and chemicals in the nation's drinking water. Today, the water that reaches your home has passed through many tests to ensure its quality.

Water Quality Test

Materials

unflavored laxative tablets, rubbing alcohol, ammonia, water, clear plastic drinking cups, eyedropper, fork

In Preparation: Before beginning this activity, you will need to make an indicator dye known as phenolphthalein. Laxative tablets contain about 90% phenolphthalein.

1. Grind up 3 unflavored laxative tablets (any brand) into a fine powder, using your fork to crush the tablets.
2. Mix the powder with 1 cup (250 mL) of rubbing alcohol.
3. Allow the solution to settle.

Procedure

1. Fill two drinking cups with water from the tap.
2. Add one drop of ammonia to one of the cups of water.
3. Smell both cups of water. Can you tell which one has the ammonia?
4. Add a few drops of phenolphthalein to each cup.

Results: The cup containing the ammonia will turn pink when the phenolphthalein is added.

Closure/Assessment

1. Does clear water necessarily mean clean water? Why or why not? _____

   _____

2. What are some of the chemicals used by water departments to treat our water? _____

   _____

Extension: You may want to purchase a water quality kit from your local drugstore to test for certain impurities in your water. Also, Carolina Biological Supply carries a number of water-quality test kits for home and classroom use. See the Related Materials section on page 47.

How Water Is Brought to Our Faucets

Ms. Frizzle and her class leave the reservoir through a pipe which leads them into the city. They are following the same journey that water takes as it leaves the treatment plant and heads off for our faucets.

Water Fact #8: *The first pipes in North America were made of hollowed-out logs. Today, pipes are made of concrete, metal, even plastic.*

As a Matter of Fact . . . In 1760, the first pumping station in the United States was built in the town of Bethlehem, Pennsylvania. A wooden pump was used to force water through pipes made of bored hemlock logs.

Build Your Own Waterworks

Materials

rubber tubing, 2 buckets, water

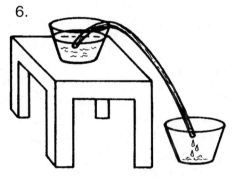

Procedure

1. Fill one of the buckets with water.

2. Place the bucket of water on a table.

3. Place the empty bucket on the floor beneath the table.

4. Completely fill the length of rubber tubing with water by submerging it in the bucket on the table.

5. Keep one end of the tubing submerged in the water. Place your thumb over the other end of the rubber tubing and remove that end from the bucket.

6. Lower this end of rubber tubing into the bucket on the floor and release your thumb. The water should begin to flow.

Results: You will now have created your own waterworks system. This basic siphon system will only work so long as the end of the hose in the empty bucket is lower than the end of the hose in the bucket full of water. If you raise the end of the hose above the bucket full of water, the siphon will stop. Lower it, and the siphon will start up again as long as there is still some water in the tubing section that is outside the bucket.

Extension: Create a series of waterworks by placing several buckets on a staircase and run siphons from one to the next.

Also, Delta Education offers an ESS kit on the properties of siphons. See the Related Materials section on page 47 for more information.

Fun Fact: *The world's longest water pipeline is in Australia. The original construction began in 1903, and today it stretches over 350 miles from the city of Perth to the Kalgoorlie goldfields.*

Water Pressure

Ms. Frizzle and her class are swept into town through the city's system of water pipes. The water pressure in the pipes forces the class under the streets and into a building.

Water Fact #9: *Water pressure is usually so strong you can't keep water from coming out of an open faucet with your finger, no matter how hard you press.*

As a Matter of Fact . . . A liquid flowing through a pipe will speed up if the pipe becomes smaller. Therefore, the children in the smaller pipe are moving faster than Ms. Frizzle, who is right behind them in the larger pipe.

Make Your Own Water Pistol

Plastic water pistols often have the smallest opening possible. This is bad if you really want to get your target wet, but it is good if you want to shoot at a target which is far away. The bigger the opening, the more pressure must be applied to get the water to go far.

Compare the streams of a tiny water pistol to that of a larger water "pump gun." You will notice the water pistol has a thinner stream of water, but the larger gun requires pumping to make its thicker stream go farther.

Materials

1 squeeze bottle of water which has a drinking nozzle
   • without nozzle   • with nozzle

Precaution: This is an outdoor activity!

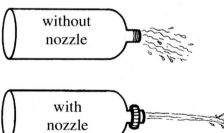

Procedure

1. Remove the nozzle and fill the bottle with water.
2. Without replacing the nozzle, point the bottle away from your body and squeeze it as hard and as fast as you can.
3. Again fill the bottle with water.
4. Screw the nozzle onto the mouth of the bottle.
5. Return to the exact spot from which you squeezed the bottle before and squeeze it as hard and as fast as you can.

Results: The water will go farther when the nozzle is in place. The nozzle reduces the opening in the bottle and forces the water to travel at a faster speed. Notice that you do not have to put as much pressure on the bottle with the nozzle to get it to go as far.

Closure/Assessment

What are two things you could do to a water hose to get the water to go farther? _____

_____

Fun Fact: *The world's tallest fountain, in Fountain Hills, Arizona, forces out water with such pressure that the 600 foot tall stream of water can reach speeds of up to 147 miles per hour.*

Waste Water

Water Fact #10: *The average city in the United States loses about $\frac{1}{5}$ of all its water through leaks.*

As a Matter of Fact . . . A big city like Chicago will lose over 150 million gallons (568 million liters) of water per day through leaks.

Appropriately, Ms. Frizzle's class ends their journey in the bathroom where much of our water supply is wasted through leaks. But although her journey ends there, the story of water is not yet complete. As was mentioned earlier, the water that enters our homes, schools, and offices must at some point be returned to the water cycle. What happens to the water after it goes down the drain or is flushed down the toilet?

Post-Reading: How to Handle Waste Water

There are two major ways people deal with their waste water—often referred to as *sewage.* One method is to treat the water in something called a *septic tank* immediately after the water leaves the building. The other method is to send the sewage through a series of underground pipes, much like those which brought the water into the building, to a *waste water treatment facility.*

Septic Tank

People who live in remote areas and away from big cities often have septic tanks. A septic tank is a concrete or steel container buried underground near the home. A pipe runs from the house to the septic tank where sewage is then deposited. Most of the solid material sinks to the bottom of the tank while clearer water and surface scum float on the top.

The surface scum and water, now called *effluent,* flows from the tank into pipes which run outward from the tank into a *leaching field.* The leaching field is an area of soil near the tank where bacteria in the ground can decompose any organic material in the effluent. After this, the water in the soil is evaporated by the sun and returned to the water cycle.

Meanwhile, the solid material at the bottom of the container is decomposed by bacteria in the septic tank and turns into either a gas or a substance called *humus.* The gas is released into the air, and the humus must be pumped out of the tank from time to time and taken to a sewage treatment plant.

People who use septic tanks must be careful with what they throw down the toilet. Not all materials can be decomposed in the tank. Special toilet paper is available which will decompose in septic tanks. Also, people who use septic tanks must flush certain chemicals and bacteria into their toilets to keep the septic tank operating properly.

Septic Tank Diagram

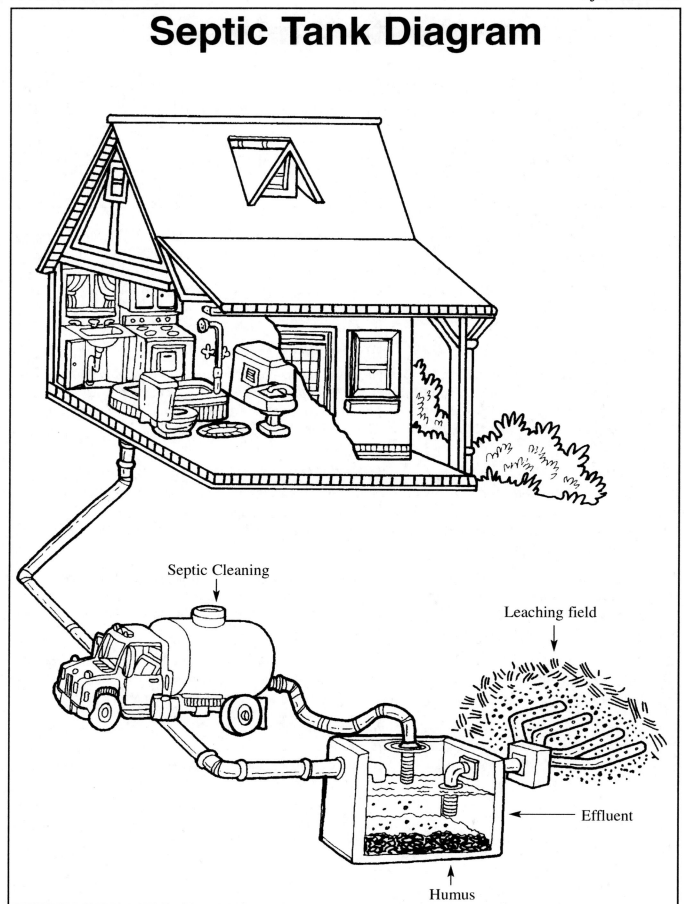

Septic Cleaning

Leaching field

Effluent

Humus

Waste Water Treatment Facilities

There are over 15,000 wastewater treatment facilities in the United States which handle the billions of gallons of sewage produced by Americans each day. Most sewage is treated with what is known as a primary and secondary treatment. But some cities require an additional tertiary (or third) treatment.

Primary Treatment

When the sewage first arrives at the treatment plant, it is passed through large *grinders* and *screens* in order to remove the larger articles such as cloth and paper. Then, the sewage is allowed to sit in order for the heavier sludge to sink towards the bottom. Between 30% and 50% of the organic wastes sink to the bottom during this process and are then carried off to the secondary treatment. The surface effluent can then either be released into a nearby water source or treated further.

Secondary Treatment

At this point, oxygen is bubbled into the sludge in what is known as an *aeration tank.* The oxygen helps bacteria grow and digest the sludge. The remaining effluent (mostly water) can then be released into a local river, lake, or ocean. Here it will re-enter the water cycle while the sludge is left behind to move on to the *digestion tank.*

In the digestion tank, the sludge is digested by bacteria which produce methane gas as a by-product. This methane gas can then be burned by the waste water treatment plant to make electricity. The remaining sludge is dried into what is known as *wet cake* and can be used to fertilize plants. As there may be heavy metals and harsh chemicals in the sludge, the wet cake will not be used to fertilize any plants intended for human consumption.

Tertiary Treatment

Sometimes the delicate water environment near the waste water treatment facility cannot handle the effluent released from the secondary treatment. This is especially true for facilities not located near a large body of water such as an ocean. In these cases, the secondary effluent undergoes a third (tertiary) treatment. Tertiary treatment is similar to the treatment given to water at a reservoir. *Alum* may be added to produce *floc,* and ultimately the water may be chlorinated. This water is almost good enough to drink! Nonetheless, tertiary treated water is either discharged back into a local water source, or is used only for irrigation (often referred to as "reclaimed water"). Currently, no waste water treatment plants produce potable (drinkable) water.

Extension Activity: Call your local waste water treatment facility and arrange a field trip. Many facilities are open to the public for organized tours.

Make a Waste-Water-Treatment Chart

Instructions: Make an overhead transparency of the following picture of a waste water treatment facility. Place the transparency on an overhead projector and project the image on a large piece of butcher paper. Trace and color the image. Hang your poster in your room.

Raw Sewage

Bar Screens

Grit Removal

To Waste Dumps

Primary Tank

Grinders

Open Tank

Secondary Tank

Sludge

Digestion Tank

Wet Cake

Alum

Floc

Fluorine   Chlorine

Tertiary Treatment

To Rivers, Lakes, Oceans, or Irrigation

What Did You Learn?

Now that you have read *The Magic School Bus® at the Waterworks* and have completed several of the exercises and activities within this book, check to see how much you have learned. Return to pages 4 and 5 and see if you can improve upon any of your answers or drawings.

In addition, the following questions are designed to determine what else you have learned while completing these exercises and activities:

1. On a separate sheet of paper, draw a rough sketch of a water filtration plant and provide an explanation of its function.

2. On a separate sheet of paper, draw a rough sketch of a waste water treatment facility and provide an explanation of its function.

3. In the space below, write five facts you learned about water from the "As a Matter of Fact . . ." sections of this book and five facts you learned from the "Fun Fact" sections of this book.

1. _____

2. _____

3. _____

4. _____

5. _____

1. _____

2. _____

3. _____

4. _____

5. _____

Related Books and Periodicals

Bosak, Susan V. *Science Is . . .* (second edition). Scholastic, 1991. This is an excellent hands-on science guide which is a source book of fascinating facts, projects, and activities.

Cole, Joanna. *The Magic School Bus® at the Waterworks*. Scholastic, 1986. This delightful book takes the reader on the first adventure with Ms. Frizzle's class to the waterworks. This work of fiction includes scientifically accurate descriptions of the behavior of water.

Evans, Barry. *Everyday Wonders*. Contemporary Books, 1993. This is a book of short essays expounding on life's everyday wonders, including water.

Harris, Mary E. "Water Treatment: Can You Purify Water for Drinking?" *Science Scope,* April 1996, pp. 10–12. This article provides a lesson on water filtration.

Jewett, Jon. "Protecting Our Water Resources." *Science Scope,* April 1996, pp. 26–27. This article provides a lesson on the water cycle.

Kauffman, Sue C. *Water Matters: Water Resources Teacher's Guide* Vol. 1. National Science Teachers Association Press, 1994. This guide has excellent ideas and activities to be performed in your classroom as you study water science. It is available through NSTA's catalog. Call NSTA at (800)722-6782 and request their book publications catalog.

Liem, Tik L. *Invitations to Science Inquiry.* Science Inquiry Enterprises, 1987. This book can be ordered through the NSTA catalog or directly from Science Inquiry Enterprises at 14358 Village View Land, Chino Hills, CA 91709. Dr. Liem's book is a comprehensive text of activities and demonstrations for any classroom teacher interested in science. *Invitations to Science Inquiry* is perhaps the best book available for activity-based science.

Thurman, Harold V. *Essentials of Oceanography,* 3rd Edition. Merril Publishing Company, 1991. This is an advanced textbook on oceanography with an excellent overview of the properties of water.

Vandas, Steve. "How Do We Treat Our Waste Water?" *Science and Children,* May 1992, pp. 18–19. This is an article dealing with the treatment of sewage.

Williams, Jack. *The Weather Book.* USA Today, 1992. This is a must-have book for any classroom. It contains colorful illustrations and simple explanations of the fundamentals of weather.

Related Materials and Associations

American Water Resources Association

5410 Grosvenor Lane, Suite 220, Bethesda, MD 20814-2192. Phone: (301)493-8600. The association provides educational materials on America's water resources.

Association of Metropolitan Sewerage Agencies

1000 Connecticut Ave. N.W., Suite 1006, Washington, DC 20036. Phone: (202)833-2672. Fax: (202)833-4657. The association provides educational materials about waste water treatment in the United States.

Carolina Biological Supply Company

2700 York Road, Burlington, NC 27215-3398. Phone: (800)334-5551. Carolina Biological carries several water testing kits in their extensive catalog of science teaching supplies. Call for a catalog.

Delta Education

P.O. Box 915 Hudson, NH 03051-0915. Phone: (800)258-1302. Among other hands-on materials carried by Delta, their Elementary Science Study (ESS) division carries a water flow kit and teachers' guide to be used to understand the actions of a siphon. Call for an ESS catalog.

Environmental Concern Inc.

P.O. Box P, St. Michaels, MD 21663. Phone: (410)745-9620. Classroom and outdoor activities dealing with wetlands are available upon request.

U.S. Geologic Survey National Water Information Clearinghouse

423 National Center, Reston, VA 22092. Educational materials and statistics of water usage in the United States are available from the clearinghouse.

Water Education Foundation

717 K Street, Suite 517, Sacramento, CA 95814-3408. Educational materials on water usage are available upon request.

Water Environment Federation

601 Wythe St., Alexandria, VA 22314-1994. Fax: (703)684-2492. e-mail: lloken@wef.org. The federation provides educational materials about water quality issues. Videos and curriculum guides are available.

Answer Key

Page 5: (pre-assessment questions)
1. There is water inside every kernel of popcorn. When the water becomes hot enough, it turns to steam and bursts the kernel into a piece of popcorn.
2. There is more salt water than fresh water on the earth.
3. Yes, there is water in the air we breathe. Breathe on a mirror to see the condensation.
4. Warm, moist air rises into the upper atmosphere where it is subjected to less air pressure. As a result, the water vapor in the air expands and cools rapidly to form tiny droplets we see as a cloud. See page 25 for a drawing of cloud formation.
5. A cloud is tiny droplets of water. These tiny droplets are kept aloft by air resistance.
6. The water evaporates into the air.
7. No. Water constantly goes through a cycle. Certain areas of the world receive little rainfall and must be careful to conserve the water they have, but ultimately, all water returns to the environment.

Page 8: (Questions Before You Begin: Moldy Bread activity)
2. Don't eat bread with mold on it. Mold contains bacteria which could make you ill.
3. A dark, warm, moist place is the best place to grow mold.

Page 9: (Ideas for bread mold—these are only suggestions.)
4. Place bread in a dark closet in a ziplock bag.
5. Place bread on a countertop where sunlight will enter the window.
6. Place bread in a ziplock bag and on a countertop where sunlight will enter the window.
7. Place bread over a bowl of water.
8. Place bread over a bowl of water in a ziplock bag.
9. Place bread over a bowl of water and leave in direct sunlight.
10. Place bread over a bowl of water in a ziplock bag.

Page 12: (Closure/Assessment: Water in Popcorn)
2. The mass of the unpopped kernels *minus* the mass of the popped kernels will *equal* the mass of water in the kernels.
4. The mass of water in the kernels *divided* by the number of kernels (100) will give the mass of water in each kernel.
6. Your weight *minus* your water weight will *equal* your nonwater weight.

Page 14: (Questions Before You Begin: The Distribution of Water on Earth)
1. 972 mL in the ocean
2. 23 mL in icecaps and glaciers
3. 4 mL underground
4. $2/3$ mL (2 drops) in lakes, rivers, and streams
5. $1/3$ mL (1 drop) in the atmosphere

Page 15: (Closure/Assessment: The Distribution of Water on Earth)
1. 2.3% of the earth's water is in icecaps and glaciers.
2. 82.1% of the earth's fresh water is in icecaps and glaciers.
3. 2.4% of the earth's fresh water is in lakes, rivers, and streams.
4. 51 degrees represents the amount of underground water.

Page 17: (Charting and Graphing: Amounts of Fresh Water on Earth)
The percentages of water in each fresh water category is as follows:
    82.1% in icecaps and glaciers
    14.3% underground
    2.4% in lakes, rivers, and streams
    1.2% in the atmosphere

Page 18: (Charting and Graphing: Amounts of Fresh Water on Earth)
The degrees in the pie chart of water distribution are as follows:
    296 in icecaps and glaciers
    51 underground
    9 in lakes, rivers, and streams
    4 in the atmosphere

Page 20: (Closure/Assessment: Melting the Cube)
1. The water went into the atmosphere.
2. No, the atmosphere absorbs the water but will return it later in the form of rain.

Page 22: (Closure/Assessment: Dew Point)
1. No.
2. The "sweat" would be colored if it came through the can.
3. Fog on a bathroom mirror, a "sweating" glass of ice water, the outside of a cold can of soda pop.
4. No, the hot cup will not allow the water vapor in the air to cool down to a liquid.
5. The cold mirror chills the hot water vapor from the shower. The vapor then forms a fog on the mirror.
6. The mirror must be colder than the dew point of the air. Since cold water has a much lower dew point, the mirror is not cold enough to condense the vapor back into a liquid.

Page 23: (Questions Before You Begin: Cloud in a Bottle)
1. See page 24 for complete explanation of how clouds form.

Page 26: (Questions Before You Begin: How Do Clouds Float While Raindrops Fall?)
1. No.
2. The rock would hit the ground before the feather. (Closure/Assessment: Procedure part 1)
The air affects the falling mist more than the falling water. (Extension: blow on the mist to cause a greater effect.)

Page 27: (Closure/Assessment: Procedure part 2)
1. Parachutes are designed to trap as much air as possible to cause air resistance. This slows the parachutist down to a more reasonable speed before landing.
2. No. Their parachutes could not catch any air to slow their descent. In fact, they would continually speed up until they hit the surface of the moon.

Page 28: (Closure/Assessment: The Water Cycle)
1. The puddle will shrink or disappear.
2. The water will go into the atmosphere.

Page 29: (Questions Before You Begin: Make Your Own Water Cycle)
1. The heat from the sun warmed the asphalt and water to create water vapor.

Page 37: (Freshwater Use: Questions for Students)
1. CA, TX, ID, IL, CO, OH, MI, NY, PA, IN are all in the top 10. Reasons: population and agriculture.
2. VI, RI, AK, NH, ME, PR, SD, VT, DE, CT are all in the bottom 10. Reasons: lack of population and/or agriculture.
3. agricultural, thermoelectric power, domestic and commercial, industrial and mining
4. landscaping, toilets, shower/baths, laundry, cooking/cleaning, dishwashing
5. landscaping (36%), toilets (20%), showers/baths (18%), laundry (14%), cooking/cleaning (8%), dishwashing (4%)

Page 38: (Closure/Assessment: Testing Water Quality)
1. Clear water is not always clean. Many impurities are too small (or colorless) for us to see with our eyes.
2. Alum, fluoride, and chlorine are three chemicals used in processing water.

Page 40: (Closure/Assessment: Make Your Own Water Pistol)
1) Decrease the size of the opening by holding your thumb over the end of the hose.
2) Increase the flow of the water by turning up the faucet.